THE COMPLETE GUIDE TO
DINOSAURS

Sandy Creek
NEW YORK

An Imprint of Sterling Publishing
1166 Avenue of The Americas
New York, NY, 10036

SANDY CREEK and the distinctive Sandy Creek logo are
registered trademarks of Barnes & Noble, Inc.

Text © 2015 by QEB Publishing, Inc.
Illustrations © 2015 by QEB Publishing, Inc.

This 2015 edition published by Sandy Creek.

ISBN: 978-1-4351-6161-0

Manufactured in China
Lot #:
4 6 8 10 9 7 5 3
12/16

THE COMPLETE GUIDE TO
DINOSAURS

DOUGAL DIXON

Sandy Creek
NEW YORK

CONTENTS

Words in **bold** are explained in the Glossary on page 138.

THE WORLD OF DINOSAURS

Discovering dinosaurs

Long before there were people on Earth, mighty dinosaurs ruled the planet. Dinosaurs and other amazing **reptiles** were the main animals on Earth for 150 million years. These creatures lived in the ancient seas, skies, and on the land.

Most dinosaurs became **extinct** 65 million years ago. This means that paleontologists, or scientists that study dinosaurs, have to figure out what they were like by looking at dinosaur **fossils**. They fit together pieces such as bones and teeth to work out what a dinosaur looked like. This can also tell us other things, like what the dinosaurs ate, how they moved, and when they lived.

Many dinosaurs had thick, pebbly skin, but some had scales like modern reptiles.

Great and small

Dinosaurs came in all shapes and sizes. The biggest were more than 100 feet long. These giants were some of the largest creatures that ever lived. Other dinosaurs were tiny and looked a bit like birds. There are more than 1,000 dinosaurs that we know about.

The group of dinosaurs called dromaeosaurs had razor-sharp claws and teeth for killing their prey.

DINO DATA

The word dinosaur means "terrible lizard." They were given this name by an English scientist named Richard Owen in 1842.

The gentle giants known as sauropods lumbered along on all fours and ate only plants.

EARLY EARTH

More than 240 million years passed between the first reptiles appearing on Earth and the death of most dinosaurs. Scientists divide Earth's long history into "periods." The three periods when dinosaurs roamed Earth are called the **Triassic**, **Jurassic**, and **Cretaceous**.

Periods apart

We often imagine hundreds of different dinosaurs all living together on Earth. In fact, different **species** of dinosaur lived at different times. For example, *Plateosaurus* died out 135 million years before *Triceratops* came along!

As the world changed, some dinosaurs had to adapt to survive in harsh desert environments.

Dinosaur planet

In the time of the dinosaurs, Earth was very different from the way it is today. In Triassic times, all the land on Earth was joined together in a single giant "supercontinent." In the Jurassic period, the great continent began to split apart. By Creataceous times, the fragments had formed most of today's **continents**.

Thousands of volcanoes formed in the Jurassic period, as the giant continent broke apart.

The changing world

Over the millions of years that dinosaurs lived, the planet changed. Thick **swamps** and forests, huge deserts, and warm seas appeared during the Jurassic period. Continents later formed as the land broke apart. Earthquakes and volcanoes affected Earth's **climate**. The sea level rose and fell. These changes affected animals and plants. Some of them **adapted**, but others died out.

DINO DATA

The whole period that dinosaurs lived on Earth is known as the Mesozoic era, or the "Age of Reptiles."

LIFE BEGINS

Life on Earth probably began in the oceans. Tiny **organisms** that were smaller than a pin head grew in the ancient seas. Over millions of years, they became larger animals.

Soft-bodied animals

The first sea creatures to emerge had no backbone or shell. They had soft bodies, like a jellyfish. These early life forms came in different shapes and sizes. Some were just blobs. Others were shaped like wavy stripes or ribbons.

The first sea creatures with shells developed about 540 million years ago. Some of these were mollusks, like today's snails.

On dry land

Eventually, animals began to move onto land. Meanwhile their bodies started to change. They grew legs instead of fins so they could move around on land. Lungs replaced **gills** so they could breathe the air. These early **amphibians** still spent part of their lives in water.

Animals with backbones

About 500 million years ago, the first animals with backbones appeared. These fishlike creatures had no jaws or teeth. They probably ate tiny animals and plants called **plankton**.

Acanthostega was one of the first four-legged animals.

Some of the early mollusks had tentacles and cone-shaped shells.

By 450 million years ago, the oceans were teeming with life, including squid-like nautiloids.

THE FIRST REPTILES

Millions of years passed. Some amphibians began to develop features that made them more suited to life on land. By 300 million years ago, these had become the first true reptiles. It was from these early animals that the great dinosaurs eventually **evolved**.

Adapting to land

Early reptiles had sturdy legs that were perfect for moving on solid ground. They snapped up insects with their strong teeth or fed on the **lush** plants that covered the planet. Unlike amphibians, which laid their soft eggs in water, early reptiles laid hard-shelled eggs that could survive on land.

Reptile eggs had a tough shell. This protected the baby inside and stopped the egg from drying out.

Scutosaurus was a large early reptile that grew up to 8 feet long.

DINO DATA

A lot of early reptiles had several rows of very sharp teeth. This helped them crush up animals like snails and grind up plants to eat.

Scientists are not sure whether *Westlothiana* was an amphibian or an early reptile.

Giant reptiles

Many early reptiles looked like modern lizards, but others were bigger, with bony **armor**, spikes, and horns. *Scutosaurus* had a massive body and a heavy, spiked head. It probably moved very slowly because it weighed so much.

SWAMP LIFE

When the first reptiles appeared, there was more **oxygen** on Earth than there is today. This helped plants and animals grow to enormous sizes. Giant plants like **horsetails**, ferns, and moss covered the land in a thick, green carpet.

Huge creatures similar to spiders lived in the murky forest undergrowth.

Fossil finds

Some amazing fossils have been found at a place called Joggins in Canada. This was once a **prehistoric** swamp. Here, inside ancient tree stumps, scientists discovered the remains of nearly 200 amphibians. These animals may have died when a forest fire swept through the swamp.

Hylonomus

Scientists at Joggins also found fossils of *Hylonomus*. This is the first known creature with a backbone that could live entirely on land. *Hylonomus* was a lizard-like animal with thick, scaly skin. Its teeth were simple spikes, but some of the front ones were longer than the rest. *Hylonomus* used these for gripping its insect **prey**.

Early reptiles such as Hylonomus had boxlike skulls.

Incredible insects

Millions of insects and spiders lived in ancient swamps and forests. These were huge compared to modern insects. Some of the most amazing creatures were giant dragonflies that were the size of birds.

The plants in warm, damp swamps provided food and shelter for insects, attracting reptiles.

DINO DATA

Venomous *prehistoric centipedes and deadly scorpions could grow up to 3 feet long!*

PARAMAMMALS

Early reptiles began to develop in different ways. A group called synapsids had a different-shaped **skull** from other reptiles. Their jaws were much more powerful and could open wide to catch larger prey. These were the **ancestors** of today's **mammals**, and are given the name "paramammals."

Many pelycosaur fossils have been found in ancient swamps in North America.

Basin lizards

Synapsids are split into two groups: the early pelycosaurs and the later therapsids. The word pelycosaur means "basin lizard." They developed about 300 million years ago. Pelycosaurs started out as small creatures. Later, they developed into much bigger, heavier, and stronger animals.

Ophiacodon's back legs were longer than its front legs, so it was probably a good runner.

Feeding habits

Pelycosaurs were good survivors. This was because each type had special teeth that suited its diet. Most had strong jaws, but they did not all feast on other land animals. Some, like *Ophiacodon*, caught fish in swamps or rivers. Others only ate plants.

As well as helping it warm up or cool down, *Edaphosaurus's* sail might have been used to attract mates or scare off enemies.

Size and shape

Different pelycosaurs had different physical features. Some of them were only a few inches long, but others grew to more than 10 feet. They looked very similar to modern lizards, but some pelycosaurs, such as *Dimetrodon* and *Edaphosaurus*, also had large "sails" on their backs.

DIMETRODON

Dimetrodon was one of the most powerful pelycosaurs. This large, meat-eating animal lived about 280 million years ago. It has been nicknamed "finback" because of its large sail.

Dimetrodon lived in North America 50 million years before the dinosaurs.

DINO DATA

Dimetrodon's sharp front teeth were good for tearing meat off its prey. It also had special teeth for grinding flesh and bone.

Warming up and cooling down

In the morning, *Dimetrodon* stood with its sail facing toward the rising Sun. The Sun would warm the sail, which warmed up its whole body. To cool down, *Dimetrodon* moved its sail to catch a cooling wind.

Top predator

Dimetrodon's name means "two types of teeth." This animal was a **carnivore** (meat-eater). It probably ate whatever it could catch. This could be insects, amphibians, and even other pelycosaurs.

Getting around

Dimetrodon's legs were not directly beneath its body. They were set on the sides. This meant that *Dimetrodon* walked close to the ground, more like a crocodile than a dinosaur.

Dimetrodon could grow to 10 feet long, and the sail on its back could be more than 3 feet tall.

Dimetrodon's sail was made of long spines that came out of its backbone.

300 MILLION YEARS AGO

Most early reptiles developed during the Permian period. This began about 300 million years ago and ended 250 million years ago.

Hot and cold

At this time, different places on Earth had very different weather. The south was cold and dry. In the middle of the "supercontinent" were huge, hot deserts. The north had extreme seasons, which ranged from very wet to very dry.

DINO DATA

Of all the species that lived in the Permian period, only 4 percent survived into the following Triassic period.

Plant-eating reptiles were common, and so were the meat-eaters that hunted them!

Reptile survival

Reptiles adapted to survive in places where amphibians could not. Amphibians needed to spend time in the water. The skin of reptiles could hold in moisture, so these animals were able to live in hot places.

The therapsid *Procynosuchus* had webbed feet, which helped it swim.

The "Great Dying"

At the end of the Permian period, nearly all life on Earth was wiped out. This is called the "Great Dying." Perhaps volcanoes pumped ash into the air, blocking out the Sun. Maybe animals could not adapt quickly enough to the changing climate. No one really knows what happened.

Some scientists think a huge volcano erupted at the end of the Permian period.

TEETH AND TUSKS

Later paramammals are called therapsids. They ranged from small, lizard-like animals to bigger creatures that looked a bit like weasels or wolves. Unlike true reptiles, some therapsids may have been covered in hair.

DINO DATA

Packs of Lycaenops ("wolf face") worked together to attack and kill prehistoric animals much larger than they were.

Moschops may have fought by head-butting each other with their huge, thick skulls.

Types of teeth

Like pelycosaurs, most therapsids had powerful jaws and very sharp teeth. They used their front teeth for attacking and tearing at their prey. Their cheek teeth were used for chopping and grinding food.

Therapsids with tusks

The therapsids *Dicynodon* and *Kannemeyeria* belonged to a group that had two strong **tusks**. Scientists call these animals dicynodonts, which means "two dog teeth." These tusks were probably used to dig up plants and roots.

Plant-eating *Dicynodon* had two tusks and a horny beak, but it had almost no other teeth.

Holes in the head

All therapsids had a pair of holes on each side of their skull, behind the eyes. These holes made the skull lighter and the jaws stronger. Once the dinosaurs evolved millions of years after the therapsids, they had a different arrangement of holes in their skulls.

REAL REPTILES

Most modern reptiles belong to a group called diapsids. These animals are very important in the history of Earth, because they are also the ancestors of the dinosaurs.

Petrolacosaurus lived in the hot, dry landscape of what is now Kansas.

Habitats

Diapsids developed features that helped them survive in different **habitats**. *Araeoscelis* had long legs, so it could run fast. This helped it catch insects like beetles in dry desert areas. *Coelurosauravus* glided from tree to tree in its forest home. *Askeptosaurus* lived in water. It had a ribbon-like tail that helped it swim.

Askeptosaurus's webbed feet were perfect for steering through water.

Coelurosauravus's "wings" were flaps of skin attached to long rib-like bones, which stretched out on the sides of its body.

Petrolacosaurus

Petrolacosaurus is the first known diapsid. It looked a lot like a modern lizard, except that its legs were longer. Its tail was as long as its body and head put together. *Petrolacosaurus* was an insect-hunter.

CHAMPSOSAURUS

Fossils of *Champsosaurus* have been found in Europe and North America. It lived in rivers, streams, and swamps in these parts of the world. Although *Champsosaurus* means "crocodile lizard," it is not a direct ancestor of modern crocodiles.

Champsosaurus swam in Cretaceous rivers with larger creatures like Trinacromerum (above).

Champsosaurus had a long body and tail, and four short legs.

Champsosaurus was quite small compared to many prehistoric beasts. Most Champsosaurus's were only about 5 feet long.

A sharp bite

Champsosaurus's long snout was filled with fine, pointed teeth, like needles. It used these to spear fish. Its jaws were incredibly strong, and its snapping bite was deadly!

Underwater life

Champsosaurus spent most of its time underwater, but would poke its snout out sometimes to breathe. This reptile swam by moving its body and tail from side to side. It held its legs tight against its body to give it a more streamlined (smoother) shape. This helped it move quickly.

Its skeleton shows that Champsosaurus's snout was thinner than a crocodile's.

LIZARDS AND SNAKES

The giant *Megalania* was far bigger than its relative, the Komodo dragon, which is the largest lizard alive today.

Lizards and snakes are the best-known reptiles today. There are more than 6,000 species of these reptiles, and they adapt well to all sorts of environments. These animals can be found in every part of the world except freezing Antarctica. They all evolved from a group of ancient diapsids.

Early lizards

Fossils of the earliest lizards were found in southern Africa. These are around 250 million years old. Most early lizards hunted insects. The lizard-like *Kuehneosaurus* had "wings" like modern flying lizards. Others were water lizards that never went on land. *Platecarpus* was a sea-living lizard that pushed itself through the water with snake like movements of its long, flat body and tail.

Kuehneosaurus escaped from its enemies by using its "wings" to glide between trees.

Pachyrhachis had the long body of a snake and the large head of a lizard.

Early snakes

Snakes are much younger than lizards. They are only about 100 million years old! They developed in the late Cretaceous period, toward the end of the Age of Reptiles. The oldest snake fossil has been found in North Africa, but snake fossils are rare because the bones of these animals are small and break very easily.

DAWN OF THE DINOSAURS

The Triassic period began about 250 million years ago, when the Earth was one giant continent. This meant that animals and plants could spread easily across the world.

A warm world

There were no frozen **ice caps** at the **North Pole** and **South Pole**, like there are today. A lot of land was desert. There was still some rain, though. Plants grew around the lakes and pools formed by the rain. This plant life attracted ancient animals.

Coelophysis probably lived in forests, hunting in packs.

Gracilisuchus was a small crocodile-like animal that could run on its back legs.

Earth changes

By the end of the Triassic period, the land was starting to break up. Two smaller continents eventually formed, with an ocean between them. The weather changed, too. As it became cooler and wetter, more and more reptiles evolved.

Triassic life

Reptiles ruled Earth during the Triassic period. Ichthyosaurs and nothosaurs swam in Triassic seas. Crocodiles and lizards hunted on land. Toward the end of this period, the dinosaurs, the greatest of all reptiles, finally appeared.

Tanystropheus's neck was much longer than its body and tail put together.

DINO DATA

The earliest dinosaurs were found in South America.

TURTLES AND TORTOISES

The testudines are a group of ancient reptiles. Today's turtles, tortoises, and terrapins are the only animals that survive from this group. In the 200 million years since they emerged on Earth, these amazing creatures have hardly changed.

The giant sea turtle Archelon had thick, rubbery skin, and legs like paddles.

Meiolania could
not withdraw
into its shell
because of its
spiky head.

Shells for protection

The testudines are different from all other reptiles. Their bodies
are inside a shell, except for the head, tail, and legs. Many
testudines can pull their heads and legs into the shell
for protection, but some ancient animals could not do
this because of the spikes on their heads.

DINO DATA

Archelon *crushed
the shells and tore
apart the soft bodies of
sea creatures with its
sharp beak.*

Colossochelys atlas's huge
legs stretched out at the
sides of its body to hold
up its massive shell.

Giant tortoises

Colossochelys atlas was the
largest tortoise ever known.
Its name means "colossal shell."
This mighty animal was about
8 feet long. Other tortoises
included *Meiolania,* which
had large spikes on its head.
Proganochelys—who lived in the
Triassic period—had a wide body
covered in about 60 bony plates.

CREATURES OF THE COAST

Over millions of years, many animals adapted to life on land. But during the Triassic period, a group of reptiles called placodonts went back to the seas. Their bodies changed again to suit life in the water.

Henodus had the same body shape as a modern turtle, as wide as it was long.

Hunting shellfish

Placodonts lived in shallow waters or on the shore. They did not go out into very deep water. Instead, they swam along the coast. They used their broad teeth to grind up the shellfish that they found there. Many placodonts had hard shells, like modern turtles. These protected their soft bodies from attack by predators.

Placodus used its front row of blunt teeth to pull shellfish off rocks.

Placochelys

Placochelys was well-adapted to life in the seas. It had a body like a turtle and was covered in tough, knobby plates. These made a protective body armor.

Placochelys had a short tail and paddle-like legs for swimming.

DINO DATA

Despite their similar appearances, Placodonts are not relatives of turtles today. They happened to evolve into the same body shape and live in similar environments.

Henodus

Henodus was a large placodont. It had a huge, square body and a small, square head, like today's turtles. Its back and belly were covered in bony plates. These protected it from attack by other sea animals such as the ichthyosaurs.

TRIASSIC SEA MONSTERS

The fish-eating nothosaurs lived and died out during the Triassic period. Scientists think they might have been a "halfway stage" between the land reptiles and the sea reptiles called plesiosaurs.

Nothosaurus's feet had five long, webbed toes.

Pistosaurus had a mouthful of sharp, pointed teeth for eating fish.

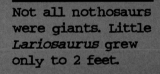

Great lengths

Nothosaurs had long, bendy bodies and tails. They stretched out their long necks to snap up passing fish. Their strong jaws and sharp teeth killed their prey instantly.

Useful flippers

Nothosaurs' front flippers were stronger than their back ones. They used their front flippers for steering, braking, and turning quickly in the water. Some nothosaurs had webbed feet with toes like a duck, but others had smoother flippers like a seal.

Pistosaurus

Pistosaurus was an unusual sea reptile. Its body was like a nothosaur's, but it flew through the water with wing-like flippers. This was how the plesiosaurs swam. Nothosaurs swam by moving their bodies from side to side. *Pistosaurus* would have snatched up fish in its powerful jaws.

Not all nothosaurs were giants. Little *Lariosaurus* grew only to 2 feet.

DINO DATA

Nothosaurs lived in the water, but they came on shore to lay their eggs and to sunbathe!

LIFE IN JURASSIC SEAS

By 200 million years ago, the world's oceans were full of life. All sorts of creatures lived in Jurassic seas. They ranged from tiny fish to giant reptiles that were bigger than a bus.

Life was brutal in the Jurassic seas, as smaller creatures were hunted by ocean predators.

Reptile hunters

In Jurassic times, life on land was harsh. Great dinosaurs hunted and killed each other. The seas were also full of predators. These included dolphin-like ichthyosaurs, long-necked plesiosaurs, and short-necked pliosaurs. Such creatures hunted fish for food.

Ammonites moved by shooting water out of a funnel-like opening in their bodies. This propelled them in the opposite direction.

Other ocean predators

Large reptiles were not the only meat-eaters in this watery world. Prehistoric sharks like *Hybodus* caught fish and **mollusks**. Shelled sea creatures called ammonites also preyed on fish. Ammonites died out 65 million years ago, but their relatives, the squid and octopus, survive today.

Hybodus sharks swam in shallow seas all over the world in Jurassic times.

DINO DATA

Some monstrous pliosaurs had heads that were almost 10 feet long!

GIANTS OF THE SEA

Huge plesiosaurs patrolled prehistoric seas. These massive creatures could grow up to 45 feet long. They had long, narrow flippers that were ideal for swimming.

DINO DATA

Plesiosaurs' jaws were full of crocodile-like teeth which were good for holding onto slippery fish!

Flying in water

Plesiosaurs did not move their flippers backward and forward like oars. Instead, they moved them up and down like the wings of a bird. These ocean giants "flew" through the water. Their "wings" were like those of a modern penguin.

Coming up for air

Reptiles cannot breathe underwater. It is likely that plesiosaurs had to come to the surface to breathe. They had small skulls and long snouts. Plesiosaurs would poke their heads out of the water to take in the air they needed.

Elasmosaurus ate fish and other swimming creatures.

Elasmosaurus

The biggest plesiosaur was *Elasmosaurus*, which lived during the Cretaceous period. Its neck was so long that it could curl sideways to make a full circle with its body. *Elasmosaurus* swam near the surface of the water. When it saw a fish, it dived underwater to grab its prey.

Cryptoclidus, from the Late Jurassic period, had teeth that locked together like a cage to trap small fish in its mouth.

41

PLESIOSAURUS

The plesiosaurs are named after *Plesiosaurus*. This was one of the earliest known members of the family. The plesiosaurs lived on Earth for 135 million years.

Twisting and turning

Plesiosaurus did not swim very fast. Instead, its body was built for maneuvering and turning quickly through water. It could use its flippers to turn sharply, and had a **flexible** neck to help snap up passing fish.

Giving birth

Recent fossil finds suggest that *Plesiosaurus* and other types of plesiosaur did not lay eggs. Instead, they gave birth to live young while swimming out at sea.

Plesiosaurus could turn on the spot by moving its flippers in a quick motion.

Plesiosaurus's nostrils were quite far back on its head, near its eyes.

42

Sea survival

Although it was quite large, *Plesiosaurus* was hunted by bigger reptiles. It had no body armor. It used its ability to turn quickly to escape from predators.

DINO DATA

Once it had caught its prey, Plesiosaurus *swallowed it whole in one great gulp.*

Body features

Like later plesiosaurs, *Plesiosaurus* had a slim body and a long neck. Its small skull was packed with sharp teeth for killing its prey. *Plesiosaurus* used its four large flippers to move through the water.

OCEAN HUNTERS

Pliosaurs first appeared around 200 million years ago, right at the start of the Jurassic period. These ocean giants died out at the same time as most dinosaurs, 65 million years ago. Like other **marine** reptiles, pliosaurs and plesiosaurs could not breathe underwater. They had to come to the surface regularly to take in air.

DINO DATA

Kronosaurus's jaws were more powerful than those of the greatest meat-eating dinosaur, Tyrannosaurus.

Liopleurodon looked a bit like a whale, with a heavy head and a thick neck.

Kronosaurus was o
largest pliosaurs.
warm, shallow wat
covered much of

Pliosaur or plesiosaur?

Pliosaurs looked a bit like plesiosaurs, but many of them were much bigger. Pliosaurs also had shorter necks and larger heads than plesiosaurs. Their back flippers were bigger and stronger than their front flippers. This meant that pliosaurs could swim faster than plesiosaurs.

Macroplata had a plesiosaur's long neck with a pliosaur's body and head, showing that the two groups were closely related

Feeding habits

Pliosaurs quickly became the tigers of the seas. They ate anything that came their way, including fish and squid. Pliosaurs also chased and killed large sea creatures such as sharks and plesiosaurs. Scientists have found some pliosaur fossils with dinosaur bones in their stomachs. Pliosaurs could not move on land, so they did not kill dinosaurs themselves. If a dead dinosaur floated out to sea, the pliosaur would snap up its remains.

ISH LIZARDS

Most ichthyosaurs were extinct by the end of the Jurassic period. Only a few survived into the Cretaceous period.

The name ichthyosaur means "fish lizard." This suits the ichthyosaurs. They lived in the water and had some fishlike features, such as their body shape, but they were actually reptiles.

With their slim bodies, many ichthyosaurs looked similar to dolphins.

Speedy swimmers

Ichthyosaurs could swim very fast. They darted through the water at over 25 miles per hour. They used their fishlike tail to move so quickly, thrashing it from side to side like a shark does today.

Big and small

The enormous *Shonisaurus* was the largest of the ichthyosaurs. This Triassic marine reptile could grow up to 50 feet long. There were several enormous types of ichthyosaur in the Triassic oceans.

Compared to the huge *Shonisaurus*, *Mixosaurus* was a tiny creature that only grew to about 3 feet. Fossils of this little ichthyosaur have been found all over the world, from China to Alaska.

The giant *Shonisaurus* only had teeth at the front of its mouth.

Deep divers

Ichthyosaurs ate fish and squid. The teeth of some early species suggests that they may also have crushed and eaten shellfish.

They could dive deeper than other marine reptiles, so they could catch prey that other ocean hunters could not reach.

ICHTHYOSAURUS

Several complete skeletons of *Ichthyosaurus* have been discovered in Germany. Fossils have also been found in other parts of Europe and in Canada. Scientists have even found fossilized *Ichthyosaurus* dung! This means that experts know a lot more about it than they do about many other prehistoric animals.

Body shape

At about 6 feet long, this early Jurassic ichthyosaur was smaller than many of its relatives. *Ichthyosaurus* had a high **fin** on its back, like a shark. Its tail fin was shaped like a half-moon, which helped it move smoothly through the water. *Ichthyosaurus* also had two sets of fins for swimming. The front pair of fins was longer than the back pair.

Senses

Ichthyosaurus had huge ear bones, so it probably had very good hearing. It listened to noises traveling through the water to help it track down its prey. With its large eyes, *Ichthyosaurus* could also see amazingly well.

Ichthyosaurus skeletons found in Germany were so detailed that the soft tissue of the fins were preserved.

Ichthyosaurus babies

Inside some *Ichthyosaurus* skeletons, scientists have found tiny bones. These are the remains of *Ichthyosaurus* babies. From this, we know that *Ichthyosaurus* did not lay eggs like most reptiles, but gave birth to live young out at sea.

MONSTER MOSASAURS

Mosasaurs were the deadliest predators in the prehistoric oceans. These giant sea lizards became extinct around 65 million years ago, but before that there may have been up to 70 different types of mosasaur. They swam in waters all over the world.

Mosasaur jaws were lined with strong teeth to bite and crush prey.

An exciting discovery

The first mosasaur was found more than 200 years ago. Some giant jaw bones were discovered in Holland. At first, experts thought they belonged to a whale. When they later realized that the bones were from a huge lizard, they called it a *Mosasaurus*—or "lizard from the Meuse river."

DINO DATA

Despite their size, mosasaurs were not always safe from attack. A mosasaur fossil has been found with a shark bite on its spine.

Mosasaur movement

Mosasaurs may have been quite fast swimmers. They moved their long tails from side to side to power themselves through the water. Their flippers were used for steering. Mosasaurs glided along the bottom of the sea, looking for prey.

The mosasaur Tylosaurus used its snout to locate food.

The biggest beast

The largest mosasaur ever discovered is *Mosasaurus hoffmanni*. This massive beast was 50 feet long. Its usual food would have been fish and squid, but it also attacked ammonites. Many ammonite shells have been found with mosasaur teeth-marks on them!

PREHISTORIC CROCS

The first crocodiles appeared on Earth 230 million years ago. Along with birds, crocodiles and their relatives are the only archosaurs, or "ruling reptiles," alive today.

Teleosaurus had heavy armor on its back, like modern crocodiles do.

Jaws and teeth

Modern crocodiles look a lot like their prehistoric ancestors. Early crocodiles had long, large skulls and powerful jaws that could snap shut. The jaw muscles attached far back on the skull so that the animal could open its mouth very wide.

On two feet

Today, crocodiles spend most of their time in water. The first crocodiles were just as happy on land, though. Some could even stand up and run on their long, slim back legs.

Protosuchus had a pair of long canine teeth at the front of its jaw.

52

Crocodile sizes

Most prehistoric crocodiles were meat-eaters, but some were more fearsome than others. *Terrestrisuchus* was only 10 inches long. At the other end of the scale was *Deinosuchus*, which grew to 50 feet.

Cretaceous crocodiles *Mahajangasuchus* attack a herd of *Rapetosaurus*.

53

FLYING REPTILES

By the end of the Triassic period, reptiles had taken to the skies. These early flying reptiles were called pterosaurs, which means "winged lizard."

On the wing

Pterosaurs flew on leathery wings, supported by an enormous fourth finger—the bones of which were as strong as those of the arm. The wings were made of skin and strips of muscle. They stretched the length of each side of the pterosaur's body. Some pterosaurs had wingspans of more than 30 feet!

When *Quetzalcoatlus*, walked on the ground, it was taller than a modern giraffe.

Two types of Pterosaur

The earliest pterosaurs were the rhamphorhynchoids. These had long narrow wings and long tails. The later forms were the pterodactyloids, with broad wings and short tails. Their diets varied from species to species—some hunted fish, some snatched insects from the sky, and some ate small animals.

DINO DATA

Pterosaurs had hollow bones, which made them very light and able to fly even though they were large animals.

Giant flier

The biggest of the pterodactyloids was
Quetzalcoatlus. This huge creature was the size
of a small airplane and weighed about 200 pounds.
It probably glided, rather than flapping its wings
like a bird. Fossils of *Quetzalcoatlus* were first
found in Texas in the 1970s.

Eudimorphodon flew low
over water, swooping down to
seize fish when it saw them.

PTERANODON

The large flying reptile *Pteranodon* lived during the late Cretaceous period. It had a small body, a short tail, and huge wings. Experts think that it may have been covered in fur.

DINO DATA

Pteranodon *had a big brain in its large head and was probably quite intelligent.*

Moving on land

Scientists have found fossil footprints of pterosaurs like *Pteranodon* close to dinosaur footprints. The footprints suggest that pterosaurs may have walked on four legs when they were on land.

Toothless feeding

Unlike many other pterosaurs, *Pteranodon* did not have any teeth. Like pelicans, it fed by scooping up fish in its jaws and then swallowing them whole.

Pteranodon had a wingspan of about 23 feet.

Take-off and flight

As a fish-eater, *Pteranodon* probably lived near water. Fossils have been found close to seas and oceans. It may have launched itself into the air from the edge of cliffs. *Pteranodon* was a skillful flyer and could travel a long way gliding on its huge wings.

Male Pteranodons were larger than females, and had a bigger and more colorful crest.

Head crest

Pteranodon had a large **crest** on the top of its head. This may have balanced or steered its short, heavy body in the air. The bright colors of the crest might also have been used to attract mates.

57

TYPES OF DINOSAUR

Scientists split dinosaurs into two groups, or "orders." The main difference between these groups was their hip bones. The saurischian dinosaurs were "lizard-hipped." The ornithischian dinosaurs were "bird-hipped."

Some theropods had big heads and jaws lined with razor-sharp teeth.

Lizard-hipped dinosaurs

The group of lizard-hipped dinosaurs included both meat-eating and plant-eating animals. The meat-eating group, called the theropods, ranged from huge monsters like *Tyrannosaurus*, down to small, scampering hunters like *Compsognathus*, who were no bigger than chickens. Huge plant-eating sauropods such as *Apatosaurus* and *Diplodocus* were also lizard-hipped dinosaurs.

Dinosaurs' legs were
straight beneath
their bodies instead
of sprawled out
to one side like
early reptiles.

Bird-hipped dinosaurs

The bird-hipped dinosaurs were all
plant-eaters. Like the lizard-hipped
dinosaurs, these animals came in
many different shapes and sizes. The
boneheaded and duckbilled dinosaurs
usually walked on their two back legs.
Armored dinosaurs like *Ankylosaurus* had
bony armor on their backs for protection.
This group also included the spiky stegosaurs
and the horned dinosaurs like *Triceratops*.

DINOSAUR DIETS

Some of the most famous dinosaurs are the killer meat-eaters, like *Tyrannosaurus*. But in fact there were many more plant-eating animals than meat-eaters in the prehistoric world.

Plant-eaters

Big plant-eaters like the sauropods could reach the tops of trees. They tore the leaves off branches with their strong teeth. They swallowed mouthfuls of leaves whole because they could not chew properly. Smaller plant-eaters munched on leaves from lower branches, or plants, such as ferns that grew on the ground.

The large sauropods used their long necks to reach fresh leaves at the tops of trees.

Meat-eaters

Only the largest hunters would have dared attack the biggest plant-eaters. Even then, they would probably have chosen a young or injured animal to attack. Smaller meat-eaters probably caught lizards and insects for most of their food. Some dinosaurs hunted in packs to bring down creatures much larger than themselves.

Ornitholestes ate lizards and frogs, as well as insects and early birds.

DINO DATA

Many plant-eating dinosaurs swallowed small rocks, which helped mush up the tough plant matter in their stomachs.

BIRDLIKE DINOSAURS

Scientists believe that birds evolved from a group of small dinosaurs called dromaeosaurs. Their name means "running lizards," and these animals could run upright on their long, slim back legs. The ornithomimids were another group of birdlike dinosaurs.

Struthiomimus had long arms and strong, curved claws.

Runners

Open plains encourage the evolution of long-legged, high-headed running animals—all the better for seeing danger coming from a long way away and escaping from it. The ornithomimids evolved an appearance and a lifestyle like modern ostriches.

Life on the plains

Ornithomimids were fast movers. Some of them could reach speeds of nearly 40 miles per hour. They lived on the plains of North America and traveled in herds.

DINO DATA

Raptors had a large, curved claw on the second toe of each foot. This might have helped them climb, as well as kill their prey.

A pair of velociraptors patrol the shore of an ancient lake looking for their next meal.

Therizinosaurus was related to the raptors. It had huge claws and a toothless mouth.

Dromaeosaurs

Dromaeosaurs are sometimes called "raptors." Although they were not big animals, they were fierce predators. They were probably the most intelligent dinosaurs ever to roam Earth. The dromaeosaurs were covered in feathers.

VELOCIRAPTOR

Velociraptor belonged to the dinosaur group dromaeosaurs, or raptors. It lived in the hot, dry regions of Asia 85 million years ago. Its name means "speedy thief."

Small but deadly

Velociraptor has a reputation as a large and terrifying killer. In fact, like most other dromaeosaurs, it was only about the size of a big chicken! *Velociraptor* was a fierce hunter. This meat-eater had a long, upturned snout containing 80 sharp, curved teeth. It also had viciously sharp claws.

We know that *Velociraptor* was feathered as we have found fossils of smaller relatives such as *Sinornithosaurus* in China, that are so well preserved feathers are clearly visible.

Fight to the death

In Mongolia, scientists found the skeletons of two dinosaurs. They had died while fighting each other. The *Velociraptor* was gripping the *Protoceratops'* head in its hands. Its clawed feet were ripping into the horned dinosaur's belly. The *Protoceratops* had crushed the *Velociraptor's* chest.

Velociraptor used to be shown as scaly and featherless. But scientists now know that its body was covered in feathers.

PACK HUNTERS

When the remains of meat-eating dinosaurs were first found, they were usually on their own. This made scientists think that dinosaurs were lone hunters. This **theory** changed as more fossils were discovered.

Fossil evidence

Deinonychus was a close relative of *Velociraptor*. The remains of more than one *Deinonychus* were found in the same place. They were close to the skeleton of a plant-eating *Tenontosaurus*. This discovery suggests that *Deinonychus* hunted its prey in packs.

Deinonychus could kill prey with the large, curved claws on its feet.

Pack attack

It was probably smaller hunting dinosaurs that attacked in packs. The clever dromaeosaurs may have worked together to bring down large plant-eaters. A group of predators would surround their victim. Some leaped onto its back, while others slashed its skin with their sharp claws.

Velociraptor hunted in packs. This meant it could hunt much bigger dinosaurs than itself.

By working together, hunters could kill even large dinosaurs like sauropods.

DINO DATA

Pack hunters would chase down their victim like hunting dogs, before making the final pounce.

KILLER GIANTS

The "lizard-hipped" dinosaurs are divided into two smaller groups— theropods and sauropods. The theropods were flesh-eating predators that walked on their back legs, including big beasts such as *Allosaurus* and *Tyrannosaurus*.

A family of horned Torosaurus guarding its nest against the huge theropod Tyrannosaurus and the little theropod Acheroraptor.

Deadly hunters

Many theropods were speedy runners that could easily catch their slower-moving, plant-eating prey. Their birdlike feet had sharp claws for holding onto flesh. As the theropods evolved, they became bigger, sharper-eyed, and more intelligent.

DINO DATA

Although their feet were similar to birds' feet, the word theropod actually means "beast-footed."

Dilophosaurus was an active hunter, that had a double crest on its head.

The True Monsters

The largest theropods include *Carcharodontosaurus* and *Giganotosaurus*. Some of these giants could grow to nearly 60 feet long. This was much bigger than even *Tyrannosaurus*.

Tiny theropods

Not all theropods were huge beasts. *Compsognathus* was about the size of a turkey. Its bones were **hollow**, so it was very light. This made it a fast hunter. *Parvicursor* was even smaller. This tiny dinosaur was only 15 inches long from nose to tail.

Little *Compsognathus* had a long neck and tail to help it balance while running.

DEINOCHIERUS

One group of dinosaurs belonging to the meat-eating line is called the ornithomimids—the bird mimics. The biggest of these was 36-foot-long, 12-foot-high *Deinochierus*. It had enormous hands, a long face like a spoonbill, and a strange hump on its back. Not much like a bird at all!

Long spines from the backbone supported a hump.

Pelecanimimus could have held its food in its throat pouch, as a pelican does today.

Ornithomimid variety

The early "pelican-mimic" ornithomimid *Pelecanimimus* was about the size of a turkey. Unlike its later relatives, it had many tiny teeth in its jaws. It also had a pouch beneath its throat like a pelican. It probably waded in shallow water and hunted fish.

A typical ornithomimid

The most typical ornithomimid was *Struthiomimus*. The name means "ostrich mimic" and indeed it was about the size of an ostrich, with long ostrich legs, and a long ostrichlike neck. It also had a toothless beak and it probably ate mostly plants, which it could grab with its long three-fingered hands.

DINO DATA

Although the *ornithomimids* belonged to the meat-eating dinosaur group, most did not even eat meat.

MASSIVE MEAT-EATERS

The allosaurs and the spinosaurs were among the largest meat-eaters in the prehistoric world. These animals lived from the Jurassic period to the Cretaceous. They lumbered across every continent in the world.

Allosaurs

The giant allosaurs had large heads on short, strong necks. In front of their eyes were two small, bony lumps. Allosaurs used their heavy tails to balance. Their short arms ended in three-clawed hands. Despite their size, allosaurs may have hunted in packs.

Allosaurus teeth marks have been found in the fossil of another dinosaur, evidence of an attack by this giant meat-eater.

Suchomimus may have walked on all fours sometimes, to support its heavy body.

Spinosaurs

Spinosaurs, such as *Suchomimus*, were also huge meat-eating dinosaurs, but they had a more unusual appearance. Some of them had backbones that grew outward to form a "sail" down their backs, similar to the sails on pelycosaurs like *Dimetrodon*. The sail may have helped them to warm up or cool down.

Suchomimus had three huge, sharp claws on each hand, which it may have used to grip its prey.

ALLOSAURUS

The enormous *Allosaurus* was about 33 feet long from head to tail. Standing on its muscular back legs, it reached 15 feet high. *Allosaurus* lived in places where there were plenty of plant-eating dinosaurs for it to feast on.

Allosaurus's jaws could open wide to tear off chunks of meat from dead animals.

A different dinosaur

Allosaurus's name means "different lizard." It was called this because its backbone was different from that of other dinosaurs. Some experts think that *Allosaurus* was a speedy hunter. Others believe that it was too big and clumsy to have hunted easily. They think it might have been a **scavenger**.

Allosaurus had three main claws on each foot and three on each hand.

There were two
bony ridges above
Allosaurus's eyes.

Big Al

In 1991, scientists found a nearly
complete fossil of an *Allosaurus*
that had died before it reached
adulthood. It measured about 25 feet
long. They called it "Big Al." The remains
showed that this Jurassic giant had
many broken bones when it was alive.
Big Al also seems to have suffered from
several infections during its life.

DINO DATA

Allosaurus
may not have been
able to run quickly,
but a single stride with
its long legs carried it
about 9 feet.

TYRANT LIZARDS

The tyrannosaurs were some of the largest meat-eaters ever. They thundered across Earth, terrorizing their prey. Their name means "tyrant lizards."

The first tyrannosaur

The first known tyrannosaur was *Guanlong*. It lived about 100 million years before *Tyrannosaurus*. *Guanlong*'s arms were longer than the arms of later tyrannosaurs and it was the size of a dog. It also had three fingers on each hand instead of two. The remains of two *Guanlong* were found together in China.

Albertosaurus had a big head and a short body, balancing on strong, pillar-like legs.

Late developers

Tyrannosaurus and its large relatives only roamed the planet for a few million years. This is a short amount of time compared to many dinosaurs. The tyrannosaurs died out 65 million years ago.

Tarbosaurus lived in Asia in
the late Cretaceous period.
Fossils of this dinosaur have
been found in Mongolia.

Hunters or scavengers?

All tyrannosaurs had huge heads,
strong legs, and tiny arms. They
looked ferocious, but their size might
have been a problem when hunting.
Their bulky bodies made it hard to
chase prey. They probably preferred
to look for dead animals to eat.

DINO DATA

*Young
tyrannosaurs may
have been covered in
feathers, which
dropped off as they
got older.*

TYRANNOSAURUS

One of the most famous dinosaurs, *Tyrannosaurus*, was a powerful prehistoric killer. At about 13 feet tall and weighing 8 tons, this was one of the mightiest meat-eaters ever to walk on Earth.

Tyrannosaurus had thick, strong teeth at the front for holding on to prey.

Big body, small arms

Like other theropods, *Tyrannosaurus* walked upright. Its back legs were large and strong. In contrast, its arms were too tiny to even reach its own mouth! The sharp claws on its hands were deadly weapons.

Ambush attacker

Tyrannosaurus would **ambush** its prey. It hid in the trees, then sneaked up on **grazing** plant-eaters. In a short burst of speed, it would rush out and grab its victim in its massive, powerful jaws. Although it was a big animal, *Tyrannosaurus* did not need to kill every day. A feast of a large plant-eating dinosaur could keep *Tyrannosaurus* going for several weeks.

Some scientists think that *Tyrannosaurus* may have scavenged for food.

DINO DATA

Tyrannosaurus's massive head could be more than 4 feet long.

Tyrannosaurus died out along with many other animals at the end of the Cretaceous period.

200 MILLION YEARS AGO

The Jurassic period lasted from 200 to 145 million years ago. This was a time of great changes on Earth. There was an explosion of new plant and animal life.

The oldest known sauropod, *Baraposaurus*, emerged in the early Jurassic.

A herd of *Brachiosaurus*, pass through a forest.

Megalosaurus's powerful jaws were armed with curved, saw-edged fangs.

The world changes—again

During the Jurassic period, the giant continent split in half. The weather became cooler and wetter than it had been in the Triassic. The dry deserts mostly disappeared. Trees grew tall, and forests began to cover the Earth.

DINO DATA

The first dinosaur bone ever discovered, was found in 1676. It belonged to the Jurassic giant Megalosaurus.

BEFORE THE SAUROPODS

Toward the end of the Triassic period, a group of dinosaurs called sauropodomorphs emerged. This group included the sauropods —great, long-necked plant-eaters. However, there were many early and more primitive types of sauropodomorph.

Mussaurus ("mouse lizard") lived in South America during the Jurassic period.

Early *Sauropodomorph features*

Sauropodomoprhs were plant-eating dinosaurs. The most primitive of them ranged from cat-sized creatures to some that were over 30 feet long. They moved about on either their hind legs or on all fours.

Anchisaurus may have moved about on two legs as well as four.

Plateosaurus's tail made up half its length.

Plateosaurus

Plateosaurus was a large example of an early sauropodomorph that lived on the plains of Europe in late Triassic times. It probably traveled in herds, looking for new feeding grounds. It moved on all four legs most of the time, but could also stand up on its back legs. This helped *Plateosaurus* feed from higher branches.

PLANT-EATING GIANTS

The sauropods were the true giants of the dinosaur world. Most of them were well over 50 feet long. The earliest sauropods appeared more than 200 million years ago.

Sauropod features

Each sauropod had a small head at the end of an extra-long neck. The body was very deep, to hold an enormous stomach. Thick, pillar-like legs with five-toed feet supported its great weight. A long, thick tail was used for balance when walking.

Brachiosaurus had a long, sloping back and an unusual dome-shaped head.

Diplodocus

Diplodocus was one of the longest sauropods. It could grow up to 85 feet from head to tail. It lived in parts of North America that were thick with plant life. *Diplodocus* had a tiny, horse-like head. Its pegshaped teeth were good for gathering up plants.

Like most other dinosaurs, sauropods reproduced by laying eggs.

APATOSAURUS

Apatosaurus emerged in the late Jurassic period. This plant-eating beast weighed as much as five adult elephants and could live to be 100 years old.

Like most sauropods, *Apatosaurus* had a long neck and a long tail.

What's in a name?

Apatosaurus was found in the late nineteenth century. At about the same time, the bones of another dinosaur were found and named *Brontosaurus*, which means "thunder lizard." This refers to the earth-shaking sound it would have made when walking. The name was later changed when scientists realized that remains of *Brontosaurus* and *Apatosaurus* were the same species. But now it seems that they might have been different after all, and so there are two similar sauropods—*Apatosaurus* and *Brontosaurus*!

Fighting for survival

Apatosaurus's great weight helped it fight off attackers. It would rear up on its back legs and crush its enemy with its heavy front legs. It could also lash out with its long, heavy tail.

Apatosaurus had claws and hooflike nails on its elephant-like feet.

DINO DATA

Apatosaurus's total body length was more than 65 feet, but its tiny head was only 22 inches long!

Finding food

Like all sauropods, *Apatosaurus* ate plants. It fed on the needles of fir and pine trees. Its long neck meant it could reach the tops of tall trees. To help digest tough plant matter, *Apatosaurus* swallowed small stones, which ground up the plants in its stomach.

CRETACEOUS EARTH

The Cretaceous period began 145 million years ago. It lasted until 65 million years ago. At the end of the Cretaceous, more than half the animals on Earth were wiped out, including most dinosaurs.

A *modern world*

During the Cretaceous period, Earth became more like it is today. The modern continents and oceans began to form as the land broke into smaller pieces. It grew colder at the North and South Poles and warmer near the **Equator**.

Some of the most amazing Cretaceous fossils have been found in the deserts of Mongolia.

Plant life

The first flowering plants began to grow in the Cretaceous period. This caused new forms of insect to develop. Some types of trees that survive today also emerged, including oak trees and maple trees.

The many new plants that developed attracted different plant-eating dinosaurs.

The small crocodile called *Bernissartia* thrived during the early Cretaceous period

Animal life

Modern reptiles such as snakes appeared in the Cretaceous period. So did small mammals. As the land broke up, the dinosaurs began to develop in different ways. They became more **diverse** as they adapted to new environments.

SPINOSAURUS

Scientists used to think that *Tyrannosaurus* was the biggest of the meat-eating dinosaurs. It has since been found that others, such as *Spinosaurus*, were much longer. 50-foot-long *Spinosaurus* was one of a group of strange fish-eating dinosaurs that existed all over the world in early Cretaceous times.

DINO DATA

Spinosaurs have been found in England, Morocco, Egypt, Thailand, and Brazil.

Like all spinosaurs, *Baryonyx* had long narrow crocodile like jaws, full of sharp pointed teeth for seizing slippery prey.

A fishy diet

The first complete spinosaur to be found was Baryonyx. It was obviously a fish-catching animal—not only did it have fish-catching teeth but there were fish scales and bones found in the stomach of its skeleton. A big claw on each hand was used for hooking fish out of the water.

The sailbacks

Most of the spinosaurs that have been discovered had spectacular sails on their backs. These sails were supported by spines jutting upwards from the backbones—hence the name of the group. On some the sail was merely a ridge along the back, but on others, like that on *Spinosaurus* itself, it was huge. *Ichthyovenator* had two sails.

Ichthyovenator, "fish hunter," had a sail on the back and a separate sail on the tail

Spinosaurus was a swimming animal. It must have swum in rivers and swamps chasing fish, similar to a crocodile today.

BIRD-HIPPED DINOSAURS

The ornithiscians, or "bird-hips," were a very successful group of dinosaurs. They survived for more than 150 million years. They began as small, agile, fast, **herbivores** (plant-eaters).

Pisanosaurus is one of the oldest known "bird-hipped" dinosaurs.

Early bird-hips

Most early bird-hips were small animals that ran upright on two slender legs. They had small heads and long tails. They also had a variety of small teeth to cut plants from branches and chew them up.

Only the jaw bones of *Echinodon* have been found, but they show it had long, sharp teeth at the front of its mouth.

Messy eaters

The earliest bird-hipped dinosaurs had mouths like lizards, which opened all the way from the snout to the jaw hinge. Later forms had cheeks, that stopped food falling out of their mouths while they chewed.

The early Jurassic bird-hipped dinosaur *Lesothosaurus* was lightly built and a fast runner.

DINO DATA

The first group of bird-hipped dinosaurs are called the ornithopods —or bird-footed because of the shape of the feet.

93

QUILLBACKS

Heterodontosaurus lived in parts of Africa about 200 million years ago. At the time, this part of the world would have been covered in hot deserts. The dinosaur probably stayed close to watering holes, as this was where plants grew.

A perfect skeleton

One of the most beautiful dinosaur skeletons ever found was that of 3-foot-long *Heterodontosaurus*. Every bone was in place, but there was no indication of what the skin covering was like.

The quills were probably used like those of a porcupine, for defence.

Teeth features

Heterodontosaurus had three different kinds of teeth. It had small, pointed teeth at the front of its upper jaw. The lower jaw formed a horny beak. Behind these were two pairs of scissor-like teeth. It used these to cut up leaves before grinding them to pieces.

A bristly covering

Pegomastax, a close relative of *Heterodontosaurus*, had porcupine-like quills covering its back and tail. The other *heterodontosaurids*, including *Heterodontosaurus* itself, probably had these as well.

Other dinosaur groups also sported quills. *Psittacosaurus*, an early member of the horned dinosaur group, had them on its tail.

DINO DATA

Quills? Feathers? Scaly skin? It is only very rarely that we find fossils of dinosaurs' outer covering.

BONEHEADS

The pachycephalosaurs, or boneheads, were a small family of plant-eating dinosaurs that lived in the Cretaceous period. They probably evolved in Asia, but later spread to North America. The boneheads moved on their two back legs and could run quickly if they were threatened by a predator.

The thick skull may have been used to head-butt rivals, or to charge head-first at predators.

Living together

Boneheaded dinosaurs probably lived together in herds. Males may have used their bony heads to butt each other's **flanks** at mating time. The animal that won these fights would mate with the females.

DINO DATA

The dinosaur with the longest name is a bonehead— Micropachycephalosaurus (my-kro-pak-ee-KEF-a-loh-SAWR-us).

Lumpy heads

Pachycephalosaur means "thick-headed lizard." These strange-looking dinosaurs had high foreheads and dome-shaped lumps on their skulls. These were made of large pieces of thick bone. Some pachycephalosaurs also had bony **frills** and knobs on their heads.

Stegoceras had one of the thickest skulls of all the pachycephalosaurs.

Head protection

A previously unknown pachycephalosaur, named *Texacephale*, was discovered in 2010. Its dome had a ridge on either side. Some scientists think that these may have acted as shock absorbers to protect the skull during head-butting.

The biggest bonehead

Pachycephalosaurus was the largest of the pachycephalosaurs. Its skull alone was 2 feet long. The enormous dome on its heads was 10 inches thick and made of solid bone. It was ringed by lots of smaller bony lumps.

LIVING IN A HERD

The fossil footprints of dinosaurs and other prehistoric animals offer clues about how they lived. Lots of footprints from the same type of dinosaur have been found together. These suggest that plant-eating dinosaurs lived in herds.

Today, animals like musk oxen protect their young by circling them, like these Triceratops may have done.

Horned herds

Horned dinosaurs like *Triceratops* might have lived in herds. They defended their babies by forming a circle around them and threatening the predator with their fierce horns.

Gathering information

Fossil footprints tell us many things about dinosaurs. Scientists can work out whether a dinosaur ran on four legs or two. They can tell how wide its body was. They can even figure out how fast a dinosaur was traveling.

Even the giant sauropods may have moved in herds for safety.

Herds of dinosaurs often left footprints in the mud around rivers and lakes.

How fossil footprints form

Imagine that a herd of dinosaurs gathers near a river or lake. They leave their footprints in the mud. These are baked hard into the Earth by the beating Sun, and later the prints are covered over by more mud. Millions of years later, the prints reappear, as the surface of the land wears away.

HERBIVOROUS HYPSILOPHODONTS

Hypsilophodonts and similar small plant-eaters lived for more than 100 million years, from the late Jurassic to the late Cretaceous periods. They spread to every continent on Earth, including the now-frozen Antarctica. When the first hypsilophodont fossils were discovered, scientists thought the bones were of a small iguanodon.

Hypsilophodonts moved through forests, hiding from predators.

DINO DATA

For many years, scientists thought that some hypsilophodonts *lived in trees!*

Watching for danger

Hypsilophodonts probably lived in herds for safety. They would always be on the lookout for danger. If they saw a predator, they could sprint away. Their long legs and light bodies allowed them to move quickly.

Cold climates

Fossils of *Leaellynasaura* have been found in Australia. In the early Cretaceous period, Australia was much closer to the South Pole than it is now, and the area was much colder. Scientists think that *Leaellynasaura* may have been warm-blooded to survive in the freezing temperatures.

Leaellynasaura had unusually large eyes to help it see during the long, dark, southern winters.

Some hypsilophodonts had a bony beak instead of teeth at the front of their jaws.

Feeding habits

Hypsilophodonts were small herbivores. The largest grew to about 6 feet long. Their teeth were just the right shape for grinding tough plants. Their cheeks stopped food from falling out of their mouths while they chewed.

IGUANODONTS

The plant-eating iguanodonts appeared about 170 million years ago. This successful group spread throughout the world. They first emerged in the middle of the Jurassic period, and thrived right through to the end of the Cretaceous.

Slow movers

Iguanodonts looked like hypsilophodonts, but they were much bigger. Some Iguanodonts grew to be 30 feet long. They had bulky, big-boned bodies and thicker legs than the hypsilophodonts. Because of their size and weight, iguanodonts probably could not move very quickly.

Ouranosaurus had a sail on its back, similar to the spinosaurs.

Grazing animals

Iguanodonts lived like some
modern plant-eating animals.
They moved in herds, looking for
good land to graze on. Iguanodonts
mainly ate low-growing plants.
They would nip off the leaves with
their beaklike jaws. Their rows
of ridged cheek teeth would
then grind the tough leaves
to a pulp.

The sense of smell
was important to
iguanodonts, and species
like *Muttaburrasaurus*
had large nostrils.

Four-legged life

Although iguanodonts could stand
on their two back legs, they spent
most of their time on all fours. They
would rear up to reach leaves on higher
branches, and when they needed to run
fast to escape from predators!

Iguanodonts had
heavy, hooflike nails
on both their front
and back feet.

103

IGUANODON

Iguanodon was one of the first dinosaurs ever to be discovered, in 1822. When the fossils were found, scientists thought it was a giant crocodile! *Iguanodon* was given its name because its teeth looked like those of the modern lizard called the iguana.

DINO DATA

Originally scientists thought that Iguanodon's spiky thumb went on the end of its nose!

Getting about

Iguanodon was one of the most widespread dinosaurs, and fossils have been found on nearly every continent. Herds of *Iguanodon* would have roamed around these lands, eating ferns and horsetails near rivers. Although they usually moved on all fours, they could also walk upright on their long legs. They used their tails for balance.

Iguanodon's spiky "thumb" might have been used as a defense against predators.

Iguanodon was about 33 feet long and weighed 3 or 4 tons.

Five fingers

At the end of each of *Iguanodon's* arms was a five-fingered hand. The first finger, or thumb, was a large spike. The dinosaur could bend this across its hand to grab and hold onto plants.

FAMILY LIFE

Scientists study fossils and look at the habits of modern animals to find out how dinosaurs behaved. One area of dinosaur behavior is how different species cared for their young.

Dinosaur eggs

Like most other reptiles, dinosaurs laid eggs. Different species laid different numbers of eggs. Some types may have laid up to 30 eggs at a time. In the harsh prehistoric world though, only a few baby dinosaurs would have survived.

Safety in numbers

It was easy for predators to attack young dinosaurs, even big baby sauropods. For safety, plant-eaters moved in herds. The young dinosaurs would travel in the middle of the herd.

Young sauropods may have put on as much weight as 7 pounds every day!

Caring for young

Certain types of dinosaurs seem to have taken great care of their babies. They would feed and watch over them in the nest, like mother birds do today. Other dinosaurs probably laid their eggs and then left them. If they survived long enough to hatch, the young dinosaurs had to fend for themselves.

Some dinosaurs may have dug burrows under the ground to keep their young safe.

DUCK-BILLED DINOSAURS

The duck-billed dinosaurs are called this because they had long, flat beaks like a duck. Their proper name is hadrosaurs, which simply means "big lizard."

Long horn

Tsintaosaurus had an unusual horn on its head. The front of the horn may have been covered with a flap of skin that stretched to its snout. The skin could have been blown up like a balloon and used to make signals to other dinosaurs.

Tsintaosaurus's horn may have been brightly colored.

Shantungosaurus lived in China in the late Cretaceous period.

Flat head

Shantungosaurus was one of the largest hadrosaurs. It had a flat head and an extra-long, flat tail. Its tail made up nearly half its total body length. *Shantungosaurus* used this to keep its heavy body balanced when walking.

Different duckbills

Hadrosaurs could be found across most of the northern world in Cretaceous times. They were one of the last types of dinosaur to evolve. Hadrosaurs all had a broad, flat snout, but they had different head features. Some, like *Hypacrosaurus*, had large crests on their heads.

Hypacrosaurus's nostrils went from its snout up through its flat, helmet shaped crest.

MAIASAURA

Thanks to an amazing fossil find, we know a lot about how the dinosaur *Maiasaura* cared for its young. This is how it earned its name, which means "good mother lizard."

An adult *Maiasaura* stayed near the eggs to make sure they came to no harm.

Fossilized eggs

In 1978, scientists found a huge *Maiasaura* nesting site in Montana. The area contained the bones of hundreds of adult *Maiasaura*, along with fossils of babies, eggs, and even nests.

An adult Maiasaura grew to 30 feet long.

Food and care

When they hatched, baby *Maiasauras* were about 1 foot long. The adult *Maiasaura* brought food to the young dinosaurs. It watched over them to keep them safe from predators.

Maiasaura nests

The nests had been made from heaps of mud. They were about 10 feet across. *Maiasaura* probably covered its eggs with earth and plants to keep them warm.

MICRORAPTOR

Some of the small theropods were so lightly built that they could actually glide through the air. They were able to do this by means of long flight-feathers on the arms and legs.

Microraptor was about the size of a pigeon. It had flight feathers on its arms and its legs—giving it four wings.

Gliders

These little dinosaurs could not fly like birds do today. They did not have the muscles for it. However, they were able to glide from tree to tree like modern flying squirrels.

Searching for food

The four-winged theropods—*Microraptor* and its relatives—hunted for insects and little tree animals in the branches of the forests. They could have swooped down out of the sky, catching their prey by surprise. Their long claws enabled them to cling to vertical tree trunks.

Furry for warmth

The covering of tiny feathers seen in *Sinosauropteryx* and other small theropods would not have developed for flight. The feathers would have evolved as insulation to keep the body at a constant temperature while they ran about, just like mammals and birds do today. Gliding and flying feathers developed from this fine covering.

The feathers of *Sinosauropteryx* were no more than an overall covering of fine down.

Changyuraptor was very similar to *Microraptor*, but much bigger—about the size of a turkey.

DINO DATA

Although gliding dinosaurs have only been found in China so far, they probably lived in all the forests of the early Cretaceous world.

THE FIRST BIRDS

The first bird

The first known bird was *Archaeopteryx*. Its fossils help us understand how birds evolved. *Archaeopteryx* had long legs, a bony tail, and clawed fingers like a dinosaur. Other *Archaeopteryx* bones were like a bird's, and it also had wing feathers.

Archaeopteryx had features of both reptiles and birds.

DINO DATA

Birds use their feathers as a display to attract a mate. It's believed dinosaurs may have done this, too.

Confuciusornis had claws on its wings and provides a strong link between dinosaurs and birds today.

Fossils of the early bird *Protopteryx* have been found in China.

Bird ancestors

More than a thousand well-preserved fossils of the crow-sized bird Confuciusornis have been found in China. It is one of the best-known birds from the Cretaceous period (145–65 million years ago). The males were distinguished by their long tail feathers.

Why feathers?

Although some dinosaurs had feathers, they could not fly. The feathers were probably for keeping warm. Modern flightless birds, like ostriches, use their feathers for warmth.

New findings

In the 1990s, scientists in China made an exciting discovery. In an area that had been buried in layers of volcanic ash, they found some dinosaur fossils that had the remains of feathers on parts of their bodies.

ATTACK AND DEFENSE

Life in the prehistoric world was all about survival. For the meat-eaters, this meant being able to catch and kill other animals. Plant-eating dinosaurs had to travel around in search of **vegetation** to eat, but they also had to defend themselves against attack.

A spiky body made it difficult for even much larger dinosaurs to kill the armored ankylosaurs.

Catching prey

Meat-eating dinosaurs had vicious claws and teeth to attack their prey, but it was not always easy to catch another dinosaur. Some meat-eaters would chase down a plant-eater, but slower-moving animals probably hid among trees and ambushed their victims.

Styracosaurus had huge horns as weapons, and an enormous neck frill for protection.

On the defensive

To make it harder for meat-eaters to kill them, many plant-eating dinosaurs had special body features. Some had bony plates like armor on their backs. Other had horns on their heads or snouts, or spikes on their bodies and tails.

Size matters

The sauropods' great size may have put off many predators. If they were attacked, sauropods may have used their long, strong tails to lash out at their attacker.

Some sauropods, like *Camarasaurus* may have had quills for extra protection against predators.

PLATES AND SPIKES

The stegosaurs were unusual-looking dinosaurs, with small heads and massive bodies. They moved on all four legs and probably could not run very fast. These plant-eaters may have lived in herds, traveling around together in search of grazing land.

Stegosaurus had four long spikes at the end of its tail

Spikes for protection

The stegosaurs had a double row of wide, bony plates down the back, one row set slightly behind the other. The rear body and heavy tail had pairs of long, sharp spikes, which could be swung at meat-eaters in self-defense.

Tuojiangosaurus had 16 pairs of plates on its back, which became more spiky over its hips.

Halfway along *Kentrosaurus's* back, its plates became vicious, sharp spikes.

Stand and fight

Unlike quicker dinosaurs, which could run away from predators, stegosaurs relied on their body armor to defend themselves. When attacked, they probably stood their ground, lashing out with their spiked tails while protected by more sharp spikes on their backs.

DINO DATA

Some scientists used to think that stegosaurs' plates might have been arranged in pairs. Now they believe they were staggered.

119

STEGOSAURUS

Stegosaurus was the biggest of the stegosaurs. This Jurassic dinosaur weighed up to 5 tons and could be 30 feet long.

Stegosaurus's plates were attached to its skin, rather than its skeleton.

Body features

There were many triangular plates set in two rows along *Stegosaurus's* back. They overlapped in two rows. At the end of its tail were four deadly spikes that it used to lash out at any meat-eater that tried to attack it.

DINO DATA

Stegosaurus's brain was only the size of a walnut, yet it was a very successful dinosaur!

What were the plates for?

Stegosaurus's back plates may have been for display, to attract a mate. The plates were filled with tiny tubes, which may have carried blood. This might have helped *Stegosaurus* warm up or cool down.

Stegosaurus used its toothy beak to tear at plants for food.

Plant-eater

Stegosaurus was a plant-eating dinosaur. It had to eat a lot of vegetation each day to maintain its massive bulk. Although it walked on four legs, it could stand on its back legs to reach higher leaves.

Stegosaurus's back legs were much longer than its front ones, so its body sloped downward from the hips.

121

ARMORED NODOSAURS

The stegosaurs began to die out toward the end of the Jurassic period. About the same time, another group of armored dinosaurs began to develop. These were called nodosaurs, and they thrived in Europe and North America during the Cretaceous period.

Sauropelta was one of the largest nodosaurs, growing to more than 20 feet long.

The plates on a Nodosaurus were covered in thick, leathery skin and horn.

Well-protected

The nodosaurs were heavy, four-legged plant-eaters. They had long, narrow skulls. Long spikes stuck out from their sides and bony plates covered their bodies. If meat-eaters wanted to kill a nodosaur, their main hope was to slash at its soft underside.

Panoplosaurus's body armor was made up of broad, square plates arranged in wide bands across its back.

A new nodosaur

In 2011, a new type of nodosaur received its name. Its fossilized remains were discovered in 1997. At less than 1 foot long, it was tiny. This was a baby nodosaur that had only just hatched. It was called *Propanoplosaurus*.

POLACANTHUS

The name *Polacanthus* means "many spikes." The dinosaur was called this because it had pairs of heavy spikes along its neck and back. It also had smaller spikes down its tail.

If attacked, *Polacanthus* would fight, using its heavy tail as a weapon.

Staying alive

Like other nodosaurs, *Polacanthus* was a slow, lumbering creature. It could not out-run a hungry meat-eater. It used its armor and spines to defend itself against an attacker.

Body shield

Polacanthus had a thick, bony shield over its hips. This was the only part of the top of its body that was not protected by spikes.

Polacanthus grew to about 13 feet long.

Guessing the rest

Scientists have not found a complete skeleton of *Polacanthus*. They only have the bones of its back legs, plates, and spikes, so they do not know what its head looked like. They guess that it was a bit like a stegosaur's head—small and narrow, with a little brain!

CLUB-TAILED DINOSAURS

The ankylosaurs were a lot like their relatives, the nodosaurs. They were all stocky plant-eaters. Like the nodosaur, it was heavily armored, but the ankylosaur had an extra weapon, a large "club" on the end of its tail. Fossils of these well-protected animals have been found on every continent except Africa.

Ankylosaurus was one of the largest in its group, weighing over 5 tons.

Ankylosaur features

The ankylosaurs were built like tanks, and some were about the same size! They had huge hips and strong legs to support their heavy bodies. The bony plates on their back and head were -thick and strong.

Male ankylosaurs may have used their club tails to fight each other to become leader of their herd

Club tails

At the tip of an ankylosaur's tail was a large ball of bone. If an ankylosaur was attacked by a meat-eating dinosaur, it would swing its tail from side to side like a club. The heavy ball could seriously hurt or even kill a predator.

Saichania probably fed on tough desert plants in its hot home in Asia.

DINO DATA

The ankylosaur Euoplocephalus *was so well-protected that it even had armored eyelids!*

127

HORNED DINOSAURS

The horned dinosaurs, or ceratopsians, became common in the late Cretaceous period. They were one of the last groups to develop before the event that killed most dinosaurs 65 million years ago.

A great range

Horned dinosaurs were all different sizes. The little *Microceratus* was just 24 inches long. Others, like *Anchisaurus* or *Chasmosaurus*, grew to be longer than 20 feet.

Protoceratops had a sharp beak and many teeth at the back of its mouth.

Horns and frills

Most ceratopsians had large skulls, with sharp, parrot-like beaks at the front. Long, pointed horns grew from the forehead or snout. A great sheet of bone, called a "frill," grew from the back of the skull. This curved upward to protect the neck and shoulders.

Teeth and jaws

Horned dinosaurs had excellent chopping teeth and powerful jaws. They could eat even the toughest plants. Ceratopsians probably lived in herds in the forests, sticking together for protection. They would browse on low-growing trees and shrubs.

The biggest ceratopsians roamed North America between 80 and 65 million years ago.

Pentaceratops had a huge neck frill that had small spines along the edges.

129

TRICERATOPS

Great herds of horned *Triceratops* lived in western North America. They survived to the end of the Cretaceous period, 65 million years ago. *Triceratops* means "three-horned face."

Great weight

Triceratops was the largest and heaviest horned dinosaur. It could weigh up to 11 tons. Its skull alone was over 6.5 feet long. It had strong legs to support its weight.

Triceratops's frill may have been to protect its neck from the jaws of predators, or as a mating display.

Rhino features

Like several other horned dinosaurs, *Triceratops* looked similar to a modern rhinoceros. When attacked, it may also have charged at its enemy like a rhinoceros does.

Feeding habits

Although it looked dangerous, *Triceratops* was a herbivore. It fed on plants and grasses that grew close to the ground. Its horny beak helped it tear the plants. Strong cheek teeth ground them up in its mouth.

Herds of *Triceratops* traveled together for safety.

THE END OF AN ERA

No one knows exactly what caused so many creatures to become extinct 65 million years ago. Some scientists think that it may have been volcanic eruptions. Others think that a huge **meteorite** crashed into Earth from space.

Meteorite impact

The remains of a massive meteorite **crater** were found in Mexico. This impact might be what killed most of the dinosaurs. The explosion would have sent a cloud of dust into the air that was thick enough to block out the Sun.

Without the Sun, plants would have died. Plant-eating animals would have slowly starved to death. Eventually, the meat-eaters that fed on them would have died out too.

The meteorite would have exploded with the force of thousands of atomic bombs.

DINO DATA

It may have taken up to 200,000 years for the pterosaurs, sea reptiles, and many dinosaurs to die out completely.

Volcanic eruptions

In the late Cretaceous period there was a lot of volcanic activity. As volcanoes erupted they would have thrown ash and dust into the air. This would have had the same effect as the meteorite impact. The Sun would have been blotted out, and slowly the animals and plants on Earth would have died out.

As the Sun was blocked out, plants and animals slowly died out.

LIFE GOES ON

Big land reptiles were not the only creatures to die out 65 million years ago. In the sea, pterosaurs, ichthyosaurs, and plesiosaurs also became extinct. Tens of thousands of species were wiped out. But some creatures survived.

What next?

Many insects, fish, frogs, crocodiles, snakes, birds, and mammals lived beyond the Cretaceous period. The next periods in Earth's history were the Paleogene and Neogene. By the end of the Neogene period, 2.6 million years ago, ape-like creatures had begun evolving into early humans.

DINO DATA

Most scientists now accept that birds are living relatives of dinosaurs, which means that dinosaurs are still all around us!

In the last Great Ice Age, there were mammals such as woolly mammoths, woolly rhinos, horses, and cave lions.

The age of mammals

The death of big dinosaurs left a gap for other large animals to fill. Mammals grew bigger, and more mammal species developed. Eventually, mammals were the most common large animals on Earth.

Some mammals took to the seas and became whales like Protocetus.

135

DINOSAUR DISCOVERIES

Much of what we know about the dinosaurs comes from fossil finds. Sometimes these are just a few bones. In other places, many bones, teeth, and even eggs are found.

Experts often have to dig deep in layers of rock to find the remains of dinosaurs.

How a fossil forms

Imagine a dinosaur dies by the bank of a muddy lake. Its flesh is eaten or rots away. Its skeleton slowly sinks into the earth. Over the years, the mud turns into solid rock. The bones of the dinosaur skeleton become stone, forming a fossil.

Fossil finds

Sometimes scientists find rocks with prints of dinosaur skin in them. Teeth are covered in hard **enamel**. They survive well as fossils. Scientists have even found dinosaur eggs with tiny skeletons inside.

Dinosaur footprints remain baked into the earth millions of years after the animals died.

Building a skeleton

Scientists study each bone to work out how they fit together. It is rare for a complete skeleton to be found, so they have to fill in the gaps themselves. They must also decide whether the dinosaur had feathers, scales, or horny beaks.

Sometimes, the imprint or remains of whole prehistoric creatures are embedded in rock.

DINO DATA

Dinosaurs are often shown as brown or gray, but some of them might have been brightly colored. Experts can only guess.

GLOSSARY

Adapted

changed in order to survive in new conditions

Agile

able to run fast and turn quickly

Ambush

to wait in hiding and then attack something by surprise

Amphibians

four-legged animals with backbones that can live on land or in water, but which usually lay their eggs in water

Ancestors

direct relations of a particular person or species of animal, but from a long time ago

Armor

special features such as thick plates made of bone, which can stop an animal from getting hurt if it is attacked

Billion

one thousand million

Carnivore

an animal that eats meat

Climate

the weather in a particular area, measured over a long period of time

Cold-blooded

an animal (such as a lizard or a snake) that cannot control its body temperature but must rely on the Sun to keep it warm

Continents

huge areas of land. Seven continents make up all the land on Earth today

Crater

a large, bowl-shaped dip in the ground

Crest

a tuft of feathers, fur, or skin on the head of a bird or other animal

Cretaceous

the period from about 150 to 65 million years ago

Digest

when food is softened up and broken down in the stomach

Diverse

very different from one another

Enamel

a smooth, hard material that covers the surface of teeth

Equator

an imaginary line round Earth that forms a great circle halfway between the North and South Poles

Evolved

changed or developed over a long period of time in a process called evolution

Extinct

no longer in existence, disappeared altogether

Fin

a paddle or wing-shaped part of a fish or other sea creature that helps it move through water

Flanks

the sides of an animal between its ribs and its hips

Flexible

something that bends easily

Fossils

the remains of dead animals or plants that have been preserved in rock over millions of years

Frills

bony plates that curve upward behind an animal's head

Gills

the parts of a fish that allow it to breathe underwater

Grazing

eating plants that grow near or on the ground

Habitats

the places in which animals or plants live

Herbivores

animals that only eat plants

Hollow

something that is empty inside

Horsetails

plants related to ferns, with upright stems and tiny leaves

Ice caps

thick coverings of ice over areas of land, like at the North and South Poles

Jurassic

the period from about 200 to 150 million years ago

Lush

something that has a lot of rich, green plant life

Mammals

four-legged animals with a backbone, which usually have hair on their bodies and give birth to live young

Marine

something that lives in the sea

GLOSSARY

Meteorite

a lump of rock from outer space that lands on Earth

Mollusks

a group of animals without a backbone, including snails and squid

North Pole

the point on Earth that is farthest north

Organisms

living things, such as plants, animals, or bacteria

Oxygen

a gas in the air that all living things need to survive

Plains

large, flat areas of land without many trees

Plankton

tiny plants and animals that live in seas or rivers

Predator

an animal that hunts and kills other animals for food

Prehistoric

all of Earth's history before humans began making written records

Prey

an animal that is hunted and eaten by another animal

Reptiles

four-legged animals with a backbone that usually lay eggs with a tough, leathery skin

Scavenger

a creature that feeds on the remains of animals that have already been killed or have died naturally

Skull

the bones of an animal's head and face

South Pole

the point on Earth that is farthest south

Species

a type of plant or animal. Members of the same species can mate and produce young that can also have babies

Swamps

areas of wet, muddy land that usually have a lot of plants growing in them

Theory

an idea that has not been proved to be true

Thrived

grew and lived successfully

Triassic

the period from about 250 to 200 million years ago

Tusks

long, pointy teeth on either side of the mouth that are used for digging or fighting

Vegetation

the plants that grow in a particular area

Venomous

an animal that injects poison into its victim by a bite or a sting

Warm-blooded

an animal such as a mammal or bird that can control its own body temperature

INDEX

INDEX